KT-551-186

Park Circus, Park Quadrant and Park Terrace, Kelvingrove.

Glasgow University, The Museum and Art Gallery, and Kelvin Hall.

Tenements and Great Western Road, Nr. St. George's Cross.

Cardonald

The Forth and Clyde Canal and Ruchill Park, with Possilpark, Parkhouse, Hawthorn and Springburn in the background.
(left)

Garngad

5

Glasgow Garden Festival — Looking from the N.W. at Prince's Basin.

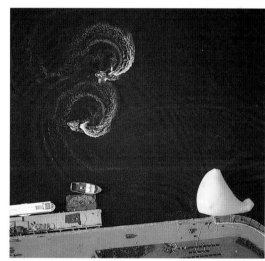

Garden Festival — detail

Glasgow Garden Festival, The River Clyde and The City. (overleaf)

The main area of the Garden Festival site.

The Tower at the Garden Festival.

The Garden Festival, River Clyde and Govan in the distance. (right)

Scottish Exhibition Centre.

Great Western Road.

Balornock.

M8 interchange at Townhead.

Partick, Dowanhill and Hillhead.

Sauchiehall Street and West End Terraces.

Looking across the city, with Dumbarton Road and Partick in the foreground.

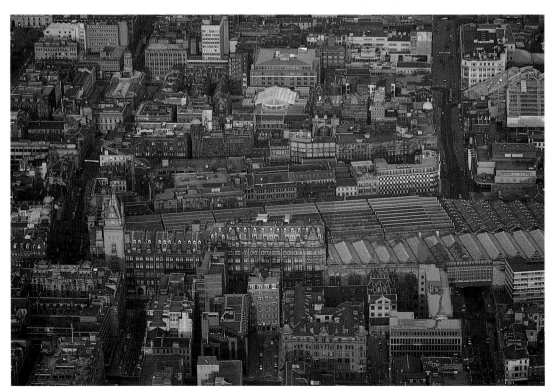

Central Station and Argyle Street, City Centre.

Paisley. (right)

The City Chambers and George Square.